CROUCHING COSTS, HIDDEN SAVINGS

10 DEADLY MOVES FOR THE FRUGAL WARRIOR

BY: BUCK FLOGGING

www.QuitN6.com

ISBN: 1-942761-77-5
ISBN-13: 978-1-942761-77-8

TABLE OF CONTENTS

INTRODUCTION

Hi. Buck Flogging here. The man. The myth. The LEGEND.

In most of my other materials my emphasis is strictly on making money. My flagship course is called "Quit Your Job in 6 Months (QuitN6 for short)," and it's all about the secrets I've uncovered that enable just about any semi-intelligent and driven person to create an online venture from scratch and get it making $100 or more per day in 6 months or less.

If you haven't checked that shit out yet, you should. Go to www.QuitN6.com and sign up.

In other Buck Flogging ventures, my specialty is helping people save a ton of money on books, courses, and other products. And in pursuit of quitting your job and being able to support yourself with an internet-only income, it's completely absurd not to address the spending part of the equation.

So I think it's long overdue that I reveal some of my frugal ninja ways. Damnit. I really didn't want to use the word "ninja" in this book. I guess it was inevitable.

While I, Buck Flogging, may portray a rich yuppie-like character on the surface, those who have followed me long enough will know that I'm really making a mockery of our society's consumeristic moneylust. To me, that shallow shit peaked in the '80s with Michael J. Fox's movie *The Secret of My Success*.

You see, I grew up in a place where the beer flows like wine and the women instinctively flock like the salmon of Capistrano. I'm talking about a little place called Aspen.

And there I got to witness some of the most vile and disgusting money-flushing that occurs on this planet. It's amazing just how much money people can waste for no good reason in pursuit of trying to seem cool and powerful. The things I've seen would absolutely nauseate any true frugal warrior.

And my friends from the local area and I never thought it was very cool or powerful. We had a blast making fun of all the dumb Joker-faced, balloon-breasted hags in their fur coats and practically kept score on who could be the most disrespectful to the celebrities that visited. My best friend was a doorman for a nice hotel and actually closed the door on Mariah Carey as she tried to walk into the hotel, haha. Classic.

Today I live off of a pretty tiny amount of money even though I don't have to, and I'm quite proud of it. Proud in a way that a rapper is proud of wearing gold medallions and being surrounded by enthusiastic twerkers.

Now, some of you may just want to save some money. That's cool. You'll get a lot out of this book. If anything you'll just have permission from a certified pro that it's okay to live differently than everyone else. You don't need the biggest mortgage you can get, and not everyone in your household over 16 needs to have their own car. College is a waste of money, yada yada. Not signing up for the typical expenses doesn't make you a poor, unfortunate soul. It just means you are making smarter decisions than everyone else—based on intelligent thought and reason rather than social programming from a barrage of movies, television, music videos, and advertisements.

Nothing to feel ashamed about. In fact, you might develop the disease, ITEMBMIFR (I think every motherfucker besides me is fucking retarded) like I have. It's a nasty disease that results in a great deal of social isolation, but I'm managing the symptoms just fine.

So, as I was saying, if you're looking to lower your expenses, this book will help you a lot. But you should know going into this book that the person writing it has an almost compulsive non-spending disorder. Every time I pull the debit card from my Bad Motherfucker wallet (a perfect replica from *Pulp Fiction*), I feel as if I just dropped a bar of soap in a crowded prison shower. It's uncomfortable. It hurts. I feel a little abused.

To me, frugality isn't just about having a more favorable net worth or saving up for one of those basic ass Caribbean cruises or some such foolishness. Rather, I consider myself a true frugal warrior. I conserve money for the same reason hippies don't flush after peeing. Because using resources when resources don't need to be used is painful and unnecessary. Like circumcision but without genital involvement.

This book is simply about adopting some practices and gaining some knowledge and a mindset that help you spend less. It's not so that you can save money to spend on something else. It's just spending less, period, for the pure sake of feeling the satisfaction of spending less. Hell, by spending less you might even be able to work less. Maybe even just quit your job and live off some rather scant internet earnings while traveling the world for half the cost of your current stale, mundane, slave-like existence!

Like I said though, how you choose to use this information is entirely up to you. You don't have to become a neurotic, obsessive weirdo living in a van down by the river like me.

Enough with the introductions though. Let's get right into some serious shit that could be crouching in the bushes, costing you hundreds of thousands of dollars over the course of your lifetime without you even realizing it. Sadly, it's often the thrifty-minded individual that loses the most money to this horrible, outdated practice: *saving money*.

Saving Money

Want to lose a bunch of money without even realizing it? By all means, save as much money as possible.

Seems like an oxymoron doesn't it? Saving money costs money. What the buck is this guy flogging about!

No, I'm not as crazy or stupid as I seem. In fact, this chapter can be used to self-diagnose craziness and stupidity. If you agree that saving money is expensive after having read this chapter, you're okay. If you disagree, you're a fucking idiot and your family should have you committed to the nearest psychiatric ward right away.

And that's because there is no debate here. What I'm about to say is the truth, and there is no wiggle room for disagreement or dissent.

Saving money is expensive as hell.

Let's say back in 1970 your parents kicked the bucket and left you some inheritance money. It was enough to buy a brand new 3,000 square foot house in the suburbs on a full acre. But instead of buying that house, you put the money into a shoebox and tucked it under your bed as your retirement money.

Good for you! You're saving money! As we all know, saving money is a wonderful thing and this goddamn great country of Ammurrica could sure use some old-fashioned saving to get us out of this doggone sluggish economy.

Ha.

Now, in 2016, you finally reach retirement age. You open that box of money up in 2016 to buy yourself that shiny dream home on that lush acre of gorgeous grass and...

Oh fuck. You don't have enough money to buy even a quarter acre in the suburbs, much less one with a great house already built on it. You might be able to put a used RV that you find on Craigslist on that tiny sliver of land, but that's about it.

Why? Because, with modern monetary policies of governments around the world, money loses a shitload of value over time.

The value of money is always changing, and, except for a few brief periods since these policies were implemented back in the early '70s, those changes are for the worse. It's like putting your money into stocks in an eternal bear market.

Yes, money is an investment. And remember this...

Money is the worst investment in the world. Ever. Money always goes down. Money always loses.

Now, I'm not saying you shouldn't save. Saving is indeed good and not old-fashioned. But don't save MONEY. Only fools save money. The immaculately wealthy use their extra money to buy stocks, commodities, precious metals, real estate, art, and other things that don't lose their value. Money loses its value.

Of course you can put your money in an interest-bearing account—your typical savings account and what have you. And yeah, that's much better than tucking cash into a shoebox or just watching it sit there in your bank account. But the yields are so low it hardly comes close to the rapid devaluation of money, and with the recent expansion of the money supply in nearly every country in the world since the economic crisis of 2008, I have every reason to believe that the devaluation of money is only going to *accelerate* in the coming decades.

The only money you should have should be in your checking account, and it should only be enough to get you through a couple of months. If you have more money than that, get rid of it! And I don't mean buy shit that loses value. Buy shit that maintains or increases its value over time compared to paper currency, which is about everything on earth except planes, cars, hoes, and fresh seafood.

Now, you may fear the stock market for example, but if you had taken that $25,000 or so that you inherited back in 1970 and put every penny into a wide range of stocks, you'd have around $660,000 now, and that would indeed be just enough to buy a nice house on an acre of green grass in most suburban areas of the U.S. and A.

Listen, the people who control most of the world's money invest. And, to win at investing (especially if you are using a lot of leverage, which is basically high-stakes gambling with more money than you actually have), it sure helps to know which way the price is going.

Modern monetary policy ensures that the price of just about everything is going up just about all of the time. Those who play the game win. It's like Vegas but with reverse odds. You're much more likely to win than lose.

With currency, you always lose. The value of all currencies is going down most of the time.

The answer is simple. Take the extra money you have and accumulate stuff that has inherent value. I use my extra money to buy silver coins. When I first bought silver coins, the price of silver was a wee $9 an ounce. It's currently at $20.69. Yeah, the value floats up and down wildly, but silver is a safer bet, and it's something you can buy little chunks at a time (investing in real estate isn't quite so easy, you need big chunks of money to play ball there).

Or you could buy stocks in the general stock market, just don't buy all the same stock. Spread it out amongst dozens of stocks in several sectors. Keep your risk low and don't make rookie investor mistakes by trying to make more than 10% per year or so on your money. Be satisfied with 10%. It adds up to a lot over time for those who are patient.

And don't pull your money in and out, buying and selling like a fucking day trader. You'll drive yourself nuts doing that and will probably end up losing everything. Just buy some stuff and let it sit for a while. Don't panic when it goes down. Only sell it when it's made a profit (unless shit is just getting ugly because of something going on with the company or the sector in the overall economy). And when you do sell it, use that money to quickly buy something else of value—holding your dollars for brief moments at the longest.

What's the worst that can happen? The worst that can happen is that you put your money into stocks, commodities, precious metals, land, etc. right before a major market crash. It could happen. But the good news is that if you are losing your ass because the price of the things you bought are plummeting, that means the price of everything else is probably plummeting as well. While you might be losing some wealth, at least gas, food, housing, and other regular expenditures of yours are shrinking along with it.

Convinced? If not, think of me when you go to the grocery store and buy a $20 loaf of bread in the year 2040. I'll be saying "told ya so."

Money ain't shit.

Your Deadly Move: Mercilessly convert excess income into valuable stuff that appreciates over time compared to the dollar.

Food

I once worked at a fishing lodge in Alaska, and when I showed up the owners had a little talk with me. What about?

Butter. Fucking butter.

They wanted to feed the lodge guests butter, but insisted I use margarine for the staff, and some weird ass cooking oil that looked like Tang sludge. God damnit what I'd give to remember the name of that stuff. It was horrifying and had a name like Whipple or something. So wrong. Yeah, like I'm going to cook with that shit. I had some dignity even back then in the my 20s.

Folks, here's what's wrong with that. Butter is one of the cheapest foods on the face of the planet. Yes, margarine is cheaper, but the battle of keeping your grocery bills down isn't won and lost on butter vs. margarine. It's won elsewhere.

Needless to say I used butter for everything all summer long. Shitloads of it. And they had a very successful season. I know for a fact that the staff and guests alike have never eaten so well before or since—much of it because I used so much fucking butter! And, while I didn't keep close track, I'm sure food costs were as low or lower than they'd ever been.

I don't have a ton to say about reducing your grocery bills, but I do have a key insight that will help you a lot. Before we get there though, let me start this chapter by shouting the obvious at a very high volume...

STOP FUCKING EATING AT RESTAURANTS!

There, that'll save you at least 80% on food costs right there. Seriously though, even fast food is outrageously expensive compared to typical groceries. For me to get the bare minimum amount of calories I need to function (take a shit every now and then, get an erection, sleep, have energy, not murder anyone, etc.), I'd need to eat at least two large extra value meals from McDonald's every day. With tax that would run me at least $16 per day, or nearly $500 a month. $500 a month for the lowest quality cheap restaurant food on the planet! It's an epic ripoff.

Speaking of calories, that's what I wanted to discuss with you in this chapter. The big deadly move for the frugal warrior is being aware of *calories per dollar* and doing a tiny bit of math from time to time.

Listen, forget about what your health guru told you. At the end of the day, no matter how many servings of fruits and vegetables you eat, or whether you eat low fat or low carb or some other retarded diet, we all gravitate towards eating about the same amount of calories per day over time. Sure, those people that have to be cut out of their bedrooms by the fire department are exceptions, but they are rare. Most of us eat a fairly reasonable amount of food.

And that amount is based mostly on the number of pounds of lean body mass you have (bones, muscle, organs), your age, and your physical activity levels.

Most adults under 30 years of age will eat 20 times their lean mass weight (in pounds) in calories per day, plus a few hundred extra for every hour of vigorous exercise.

So if you weigh 200 pounds, and you have 20% body fat, then you have roughly 160 pounds of lean mass. So that's 3,200 calories per day if you aren't very active.

As you age, you'll eat about 1% less with each passing year after 30. You also tend to lose lean mass as you age and have a reduced desire for physical activity, and eat even less.

But all that talk isn't really the focus of this book. Just know that no matter what foods you select at the grocery store for yourself, at the end of the day what you are doing is exchanging dollars for calories. Plain and simple. Don't shop by the pound. Shop by calories per dollar. The more calories per dollar the cheaper the food.

This puts things into an entirely new perspective. Butter has roughly 800 calories per pound. It's one of the cheapest foods on the planet. At the fishing lodge I served everyone a lot more butter and a lot less expensive meat and vegetables (which can often be less than 100 calories per dollar). I'd give them 3-4 ounce portions of those expensive meats (about half the typical serving size at most restaurants), and keep the meal rich and buttery. They would be full and satisfied and rave about the food. The owners were happy and didn't force me to cook with weird shit, as I actually reduced their food costs significantly despite ordering 2-3 times more butter than prior chefs they had at the lodge.

With butter, everyone wins.

Okay, enough of that silliness. Obviously you don't want to try to live off of butter alone or you won't have a very good time. But if you like it and it seems to treat you well, you're perfectly fine to buy and eat it without losing any of your frugal warrior powers.

Other foods that have a lot of calories per dollar include your typical starchy staples: rice, oats, beans, pasta, flour, cornmeal, and so on. Starchy staple foods have been the centerpiece of the human diet for 10,000 years. Many believe that eating in such a way confers tremendous health benefits. Let's not get too carried away, but I think it's perfectly fine for most to eat a lot of these foods, and they are outrageously cheap.

For example, I'm looking at the nutrition label on about a $20 bag of Jasmine rice. Figuring out the number of calories per dollar in a food like this is easy. Just multiply the number of calories per serving times the number of servings in the container. That's the total amount of calories in the whole thing. In the case of this big ass bag of rice, that's 160 calories per serving X 202 servings per container = 32,320 calories.

At $20 for the whole thing (it might have been a little less I can't remember, but that's close), that's over 1,600 calories per dollar! Now that's some cheap eats! I could get the calories I need for just $2 per day with rice. Other varieties and quantities of rice are even cheaper.

Now, how do you feel when you go to buy olive oil and it's like $15. It kind of hurts right? It seems expensive. But is it? Hell no. It's even cheaper than butter. Over 1,000 calories per dollar.

Okay, so fats, dry starches, sugar, butter, and oil are really cheap. That shouldn't be a huge surprise. But what about everything else?

For meats, seafood, and dairy products, usually the higher the fat content the more calories you get per dollar. Chicken may seem like the cheapest meat, but it's absolutely not. Especially skinless breasts. Ground beef with a high fat content is downright reasonable. Pork, except for maybe the tenderloin, is practically free. Skim milk is a total ripoff, but whole milk is a steal. Seafood might have seemed expensive to you before, but wait until you do some calories per dollar calculations on it. Time to get a fishing rod motherfucker!

For vegetables, starchy root vegetables like potatoes, sweet potatoes, yucca, and yams are your cheapest options. Onions, carrots, turnips, and parsnips are fairly reasonable as well. Of course, you should probably buy a few vegetables to add to your diet even though they are extremely expensive. But no need to overdo it. Those who choke down the most vegetables on some weird diet usually just end up farting a lot and throwing a ton of money away at farmer's markets and Whole Foods. If you like farting though, by all means, fill up a punchbowl with salad greens and go to town.

Fruit, dried fruit, and fruit juice tends to be cheaper than most non-starchy vegetables, but everything but bananas and orange juice are pretty expensive. Again, price shouldn't be your only consideration, but if you only had $300 per month to spend on groceries, you'd starve to death trying to eat Honeycrisp apples on that budget.

Another hilarious thing I see people freak out about unnecessarily is salt. The cheap shit is like $1.50 and the expensive shit is like $8. How many times do you buy salt in a year? Really? Twice? I think it's okay to get the expensive kind if you want. It won't break the budget at just a few extra pennies per day. Your salt-buying decision certainly isn't something to stress over.

Another class of foods I haven't discussed are nuts and seeds, including peanuts. Don't let the price per pound fool you. These foods, which are very calorie-dense, are typically quite reasonable on a calories per dollar basis.

Lastly, before we move on from the topic of food, know that most prepared foods are much more expensive on a calories per dollar basis than foods in their crude form. Flavored rice dinners are much more expensive than rice itself. Breakfast cereal, made from oats, wheat, sugar, and corn mostly, are a lot more expensive than oats, wheat, sugar, and corn by themselves.

The exception is Ramen noodles. Fuckin' A I'll never figure out how those things are so damn cheap. They have a reputation for being inexpensive, and that reputation is well-deserved. Usually you can buy 4-5 packets per dollar, each one containing nearly 400 calories. That's 1,600-2,000 calories per dollar! While Ramen noodles are some pretty slummin' ass non-nutritive stuff, you can't argue with their insane value and ease of preparation. Can I get a Ramen?

Sorry, that's been overdone. Hey, what I lack in originality I make up for in vulgarity. That's what counts.

So, how do I shop? Well I certainly don't walk through the supermarket with a calculator and obsessively read every label. I'm not trying to hit some exact food budget each month. But what this insight can give you is a general sense. Oil is cheaper than butter. Butter is cheaper than chicken. Whole milk is cheaper than skim milk. Rice is cheaper than potatoes. Potatoes are cheaper than broccoli. And so on.

Also be sure to see how some of your favorite packaged foods, snack foods, drinks, etc. measure up, as well as the restaurant food you buy. You may discover that foods you thought were cheap aren't, and vice versa.

I like to buy mostly foods that I know are around 300 or more calories per dollar with the exception of a few fruits and vegetables, as well as spices and seasonings including salt. I eat a little over 3,000 calories per day, so choosing these foods is guaranteed to put me under $300 per month in personal grocery bills. Not rice, beans, oats, Ramen, sugar, and oil low, which could feed a human for just a couple bucks a day. But low enough to beat your typical Western diet eater by a large margin.

So yeah, maybe get the calculator out a few times at home with some of your favorite foods. See what the real cost of those foods is. Sneak a few calculations away in your mental database. And shop more wisely.

Food is one of the eight major expenditures in our lives. I hope this chapter saves you some coin. While we could talk all day about perishables vs. nonperishables and reducing food waste, frozen vs. fresh, and a number of other topics, there is only one major revelation I really wanted to share with you. And that, of course, is grocery shopping based on calories per dollar.

Oh, and one last thing. If you find it too mathematically challenging to calculate calories per dollar, I have a suggestion:

With your right hand, bundle all five of your fingertips together like you were holding the leafy part of a strawberry between them. Now dip your fingertips into Sriracha sauce, followed by plunging all five of your fingers, up to the second knuckle, directly into your rectum. Keep them there indefinitely.

While this won't actually help you with your calculations, it will make you look like a fucking idiot, which will help the rest of us identify you and thus employ a barrage of contraceptive methods if we feel inspired to fuck you (unlikely).

Next let's talk about something a little more interesting and fun. Vroom vroom!

Your Deadly Move: Shop by calories per dollar, not dollars per pound—and the only time you should eat out is when there's a crotch in your face.

CARS

"*Don't buy a new car! It loses like $5,000 in value the moment you drive off the lot!*"

Yeah, we've all heard that one. And in this situation, the conventional wisdom is pretty spot on. There are some SERIOUS crouching costs in the automotive world. Hopefully this chapter will have you thinking clearly and making better car-buying decisions.

Firstly, let's ask the most obvious question. Do you really need a car? The cost of owning and operating even a normal car, truck, or SUV can easily exceed $500 and become a very major expense. You better make sure you actually need one.

Do you live in a city with good public transportation and services like Lyft and Uber? How often do you leave town to go on a trip? Could you fly there instead? Could you rent a car? Can you share a car with a roommate, friend, family member, neighbor, or spouse? I'd say half of the people who own cars could still live their lives as they are without a car, and do so for less money. In some cases far less money.

But whether or not you can make do without a car is up to you. Most think they can't, but take their car away and they find out how to navigate public transportation, bum rides, and so forth very quickly—only to discover they didn't really need a car that badly after all. I commend those of you who dare give this a try. Ditching a car is some serious frugal sensei shit.

Certainly you didn't grab this book for lame advice like, "Save money on cars by getting rid of your car!" So let's move on.

Here's the thing about cars: Everyone puts way too much focus on their monthly payment, as if that's all that mattered in the world. The ones the don't often put their focus on even more irrelevant things, like fuel economy or maintenance costs.

Sure, you have to be able to squeeze your monthly car payment into your monthly income somehow. But there is so much more going on without you even realizing it, and those goings on are far more significant to your overall financial well-being than your monthly payment.

A wiser car shopper will look at all the costs and think about the overall money lost from having owned the car for many years. They will then take this information and buy the right vehicle instead of the brand new XLRT Sport 2000 GT McYupppiemobile.

Believe it or not, but in the 22 years I've owned and operated automobiles, I've bought and sold 13! I'm a regular pro at it. I've even bought cars, drove them, and then sold them for more (significantly more with a Kia I once owned) than I paid for them many months later. But I've made mistakes, too. I know, it's hard to believe. Here's what I've learned...

Firstly, I can say definitively that your monthly car payment don't mean shit. Think about it this way. Your monthly car payment is say, $300 on a $15,000 car. Your APR on the loan for the car is 4%. That means the most you'll pay in interest in a year is $600, and the interest will get smaller and smaller over time while your monthly payment remains the same.

So, worst case, you pay $3,600 per year, $600 is interest and $3,000 goes towards the principal balance. What's happening here? Basically, you're losing $50 a month for the first year (I know my math isn't exact, this is just to get a concept across you fucking geek), and the other $250 of your $300 payment is the equivalent of a balance transfer from one account to another. You are trading $250 of cash for $250 of an asset. No money is lost there.

Seriously. It's not a $300 expense. At all. And as the life of the loan goes on into the 2nd year, 3rd year, and so on, the amount you're losing to interest keeps getting more and more trivial.

The monthly amount you pay, and the price of the car, while relevant, aren't as relevant as the biggest cost by far. That's depreciation.

Take for example the most expensive car I ever owned—a brand new 2009 Mini Cooper. At the time, Mini did this funky financing thing where they financed part of the vehicle cost, but not the whole thing. It was kind of like a halfway point between buying and leasing (fuck leasing, that's all you need to know). It enabled me to walk off the lot with a car I couldn't otherwise afford the monthly payments on, and drive cross country to surprise my young, blonde girlfriend (the most expensive thing I ever "owned" in my life by far!).

$210 a month with a 0.9% APR! For a brand new car! I was sold.

Then, three years later, after driving the absolute shit out of it (Hey, it got 40 miles per gallon, so I drove it way more than I normally would, offsetting any potential fuel savings, haha), the thing had depreciated by over $11,000!

While I had only paid $210 per month for 36 months, I had secretly and unknowingly paid over $300 per month in lost personal wealth. Sneaky I tellz ya.

And, frighteningly enough, I probably lost a lot less money owning this car than most people do with theirs. Mini Coopers hold their value much better than other cars, they get great gas mileage, I had no maintenance costs as the thing was under warranty, insurance wasn't too outrageous, and so on.

Overall, between fuel, depreciation, insurance, one set of new tires, and interest, that car cost me a little over $550 per month to own and operate.

Now, what will shock you is that the vehicle I own now is costing me far less, and it's a fucking HUMMER!

No joke. I have a Hummer H3 (the little one, it's basically the equivalent of a Jeep Rubicon or something, not one like Arnold's).

I bought it used (well, I financed it with a monthly payment of $479), and because they are no longer made, the depreciation costs are TINY. It's amazing. I check the blue book value every year and it's less than $1,000 less than it was the year before. I lose maybe $80 in depreciation costs per month, tops.

Tires? More expensive for sure but still not bad. They cost me about $15 per month. Same for maintenance. Even though it's used and had 72,000 miles on it when I drove it off the lot, the maintenance costs are fairly small in the grand scheme of things, which is typical. People get way too skittish about maintenance costs and do completely irrational things, like buy a new car because it has a warranty. I get it, but not having to worry about maintenance costs is a luxury, and luxuries'll cost ya.

And gas? Wouldn't you know that although it gets a measly 17 miles per gallon, I drive it literally HALF as much as I did the Mini Cooper, and with gas costs lower now than they were several years ago, I literally spend the exact same amount of money on gas per month!

Overall, all things considered, it costs me about $400 per month. Still expensive, and far from being as cheap as the $3,850 Geo Metro I bought in 2000 and drove for over 100,000 miles, or the Kia I bought for $6,500 and resold to someone for $7,400, or the Isuzu Amigo I drove for six months and sold for the exact same price I paid for it, but for that price it's a hell of a machine to have out on rough mountain roads where it spends much of its time.

My advice? Get the best car you can that has depreciated its balls off (like the schnazzy BMW SUV my dad bought recently for just $5,500), or get a car that is known for not depreciating. El Camino for the fucking win!

Keep an eye on fuel economy of course, but don't let that fully guide your buying decision. Unless gas gets above $10 a gallon, it will still be a much smaller car-operating expense than depreciation costs on most vehicles.

And hey, don't turn a blind eye to my boy Elon over at Tesla. Those cars, as of now, don't depreciate much at all even when you drive them off the lot brand new. When those $35,000-ish models come rolling out in a couple years, I'm going to seriously consider one. With negligible fuel costs and very little depreciation, those fuckers might just be less expensive to operate than what I have now. Don't let the high sticker price or monthly payment fool ya!

Just watch out for the type of people you attract driving around a Tesla though. Your grocery bills from Whole Foods will be outrageous! Those Tesla sluts all eat like fucking Orangutans! And their farts, in that well-sealed vacuum of an interior that is a Tesla, will have the autopilot intentionally driving off cliffs to keep from having to endure them!

Well that was a fun topic. Let's move onto something horribly painful to wipe those smiles off of our faces. Debt.

Your Deadly Move: Stop obsessing over fuel economy, warranties, and your monthly car payment—and focus instead on buying a car that's already done most of its depreciating before you buy it.

DEBT

Debt is kind of like a rather small penis (I hear. I can't even imagine what it must be like to have a small penis). It's not something you intentionally want or seek out, but, if you use it wisely, you can make magic happen.

All things considered, I'm kind of a fan of debt. And those that spaz the fuck out trying to pay it off, or treat debt like a monster instead of a tool, bother me.

So you can only imagine how I felt when a close family friend of mine married Dave Ramsey's daughter. Dave Ramsey is perhaps the world's preeminent fucknut. I once made it through about ten minutes of his show (if you don't know Dave, he gives out "financial advice," and is wildly popular in the American South where critical thinking is frowned upon). And in those ten minutes he literally told some dude asking for advice on buying a house to save up the $20,000 extra he was making per year, and then he'd be able to buy a $200,000 house in 10 years.

Wow, dream big!

Holy shit I've never heard anything so horrifying in my life. In 10 years that $200,000 probably won't buy a fucking trailer, much less a house.

A house is a fantastic investment. You can buy a $200,000 house, which is basically buying a $200,000 asset, and you can do it, in many cases, with only 3% down. Imagine buying $200,000 worth of stocks or $200,000 worth of silver for $6,000, and the risk of loaning out that money is 97% on the financial institution that lent the money. If it goes up in value, you get to keep it all.

Sign me up.

That guy could probably get himself a $200,000 house NOW.

In ten years, the house will probably be worth at least $300,000 with current trends, and it could be worth much more than that with the way money is ever in decline.

So, in essence, he's able to make $100,000 net gain on $6,000 down. That's 1,666 fucking percent!

And then, he could buy $20,000 worth of stocks, precious metals, and other appreciating assets each year for the next nine years with his extra income, probably also accumulating another $300,000-400,000.

Boom, ten years later this guy has at least a half million in assets instead of a lousy $200,000 "house" that he buys with his ever-depreciating cash.

Okay, let's wrap up that tangent. Fuck Dave Ramsey. That's all you need to know. We'll discuss more housing-related stuff later in the book.

Now let's talk more specifically about debt...

Debt can be a friend, and debt can be an enemy. Before we talk about the crouching cost of debt that you may not be aware of, let's continue to discuss the friendly side of debt.

I have some debt. Quite a bit actually. Most of it comes from the early days of really trying to make it as a full-time internet stallion.

I didn't make anywhere near enough money to support myself, so, instead of going out and working a lot to pay the bills—taking precious time, energy, and focus away from building my online enterprise—I relied on debt to float me through the hard times and get me to where my head was above water.

Including the car I financed, I managed to accumulate a solid $60,000 of debt. Collectively, I pay around 8% per year in interest on that debt. Roughly $4,800. $400 per month lost to interest.

Yet, I managed to turn that debt into a thriving enterprise, which led to further thriving enterprises, to the point where my websites combined did over $250,000 in revenue in the first quarter of 2016.

Would this have happened without the help of debt? Maybe. But debt surely helped speed things along, and I'm quite pleased. I love you, debt.

And this brings up the most important thing about debt, which is what you use it for. Did you wrack up a bunch of debt in the form of student loans to pay your way through medical school, and now you're working as a doctor hauling in $200,000 per year? Well fuck yeah man. Debt was worth it. Going into debt was the right thing to do.

But taking on debt rarely works out this well for everyone else. Usually debt is the result of buying a bunch of dumb shit on a credit card when you were too young to fully comprehend the enslavement that debt can put us under in certain circumstances (such as being young and making a measly $10 per hour).

Or, as I've heard from many in their late teens, their parents eagerly signed them up for as much student loan financing as possible, which sounded good to us as 18-year olds, but is a pretty shitty deal for those of us who went to college just to go to college—not for some specific reason to enter a specific, high-paying profession the moment we finished. Only now, many years later, do we realize we should have never got those student loans. Maybe skipped college altogether.

Debt is really a Jekyll and Hyde kind of thing. Like I said, it can be your friend or your enemy. It can be accumulated for good reasons or for completely fickle ones. Ultimately, if you run your own business and know how you could take money and turn it into more money, then by all means, borrow as much money as possible and don't be the weak-minded type that can't sleep at night because of the increasing monthly payments you're struck with.

I personally have a love-hate relationship with debt. Yeah, I suppose if someone offered to loan me $100,000 at 5% tomorrow, I'd eagerly take it. With $100,000 I could launch a website or two and have them both making a $10,000/month profit in a matter of months. I'd be a fool to turn down capital since I know exactly what I could do with it that could beat the shit out of 5%.

But at the same time, I've been feeling a little but-thurt about debt lately as I've been refocusing so much on reviving my former frugal ways.

You see, I've been feeling like ass whenever I work too much. I enjoy working. A lot. Too much in fact. I have a tendency to overdo it. And, over the last decade since working on my own websites, which is the most addictive thing I've ever done, I pretty much burned myself out. I'm sure I'll recover, but recovery hasn't been quick or easy. It's made me want to set myself up well for a future with a very modest income.

Sure, I choose a modest income for myself now, but someday it may not be a choice. It may be forced upon me, and that's a discomfort that I want to create a lot of padding to endure.

Without further ado, here's the crouching cost that's been nibbling out my ankles like a Himalayan leech...

Now, don't cringe, or thinketh of me as a frugality imposter, but including my car payment, I pay about $1,500 per month towards all of my accumulated debts and things that I have financed. The interest rates on those are pretty small. Well over two-thirds of that $1,500 per month pays down my outstanding debt. It's essentially a balance transfer. No real wealth is lost except for around $400 per month in interest.

Now, with the money I basically borrowed, I made a lot more money than what I pay in interest. It was a good deal. I'm glad I accumulated that debt. It has made me very successful.

However, what really chaps my ass is that I have to pay myself, out of my business, an additional $1,500 per month to cover those debt payments. And what sucks is that the extra income I pull out costs me a shitload in extra tax liability. While I may pay $400 per month in interest, *I pay another $400 in tax on the extra income I have to pull out to make those payments!*

So I'm really losing more like $800 per month. Fucked up right?

Essentially, my debt is costing me TWICE as much as it seems to be on the surface. I hate it. And you better believe I hate paying taxes as well. I don't mind making debt payments. At least debt has done something for me but taxes? Ewww.

And so, for this reason and a handful of others, I actually plan on selling off a few of my sites. Hoping to get close to $400,000 for them. If I did, I'd owe 20% in capital gains tax, which is a lower rate than what I get taxed on the small salary I pull for myself each month. So I could live with that.

But seriously, should I pay off those debts to save $800 per month? Couldn't I take that money and make far more than $800 per month from it? I have some decisions to make for sure, but I think I might go the frugal route, cut my expenses back to next to nothing per month, take a monthly salary so small I won't owe any tax on it, and essentially live off of the money made from the sale of the sites for a decade or more. In fact, if I were to maximize my frugal prowess, I'm sure I could live off that for the rest of my life (40-50 years I hope).

That may sound silly, but, monthly debt payments aside, I'll have a few months this year with personal expenses below $600 (about $200 on gas and car insurance, $200 on food, and $200 on satellite internet that I use out in the Wilderness). And those months, spent camping and backpacking in my favorite places, will probably be my best months of the year. Makes me think.

So, in conclusion, be careful with your debts. If you are going to borrow money or finance something, you better be sure that you'll be able to outperform both the money lost to interest each month AND the extra taxes you'll have to pay on the additional income you have to make to pay those debts (the crouching cost of debt).

As a final word on debt, a wise man once told me that it's a mistake to focus on paying down debt. Mentally, and emotionally, it's better to put your debt payments on autopay and forget them while focusing on accumulating wealth instead.

I love frugality for frugality's sake, but that advice sounds pretty correct to me. In your frugality exploits, be sure to keep everything in perspective and make the right choices based on rational logic, not a religious fervency about having a low monthly budget.

Next let's talk about that goddamn electronic bullshit. I'm sure you agree, it's way too expensive.

Your Deadly Move: Use debt wisely, or eliminate it without warning.

PHONE, TV AND INTERNET

Good old phone, tv, and internet. I've managed to live without television for 20 years. And, until last week, I had gone the last 3 years without a phone. My girlfriend and I just shared one. Plus I had a Skype number, and people could call me just like normal from anywhere in the world, and it only cost me $2.99 per month. Fortunately, when I recently added a phone, I was able to do so and even lower our monthly bill a tad. And then of course internet. I've paid some hefty internet bills since I became an internet diva I admit, but it's a business expense and not a personal one, so I feel a little more at ease about it.

Did you just read that paragraph? I hope so, because most people think that you need phone, tv, and internet. And that's just not the case. We survived without any of this shit for millions of years, and I could make a strong argument that these new additions to our lives have actually made our quality of life worse, not better.

Firstly, you better have something that you do that you can call a business. I don't care if it's blogging and you make $20 a month. You need something to make these expenses fully tax deductible. I'm talking phone and internet.

As for television, it's hard for me to even relate to paying for television. Shit, I'd never get anything done! That's why I've never let it into my house in any place I've lived since I left the nest. Maybe some rented movies and such, but television? A big monthly expense? No fucking way man. You're better than that. Life's too short to even spend much time watching television, much less pay for it as well.

So, how do you save big on these three combined expenses?

Well, they now combine television and internet together, and it costs about the same as internet-only. And, the good news about getting good quality, unlimited internet in your home is that you can connect your phone to the wifi and use as much data as you like without any extra charge. And I think that's where you can save the most money, as cell phone bills are pretty ridiculous—usually more than internet and tv combined and for what?

Here's what I would do if I was forced to live in a house or apartment and live a semi-normal life:

Get a prepaid phone with very little data and hardly any minutes. Seriously get the cheapest ass shit you can find. Make it something that you can keep with you when you are not connected to wifi at home or work or wherever else you are. Something you have for emergencies. Something you have for unusual circumstances. And something you can text message with when you're away from home.

Then, download Skype on that thing and get a Skype number, which, when I set it up, was $2.99 a month. Not sure what the deal is now. Don't pass out your cell number freely. Pass out your Skype number. At home or at work, while connected to wifi, talk on the phone via Skype to your heart's content. It will never cost you more than $2.99 a month.

Discourage people from texting you. Steer them towards email. Call me old school, but I'm an email fanatic. I absolutely love having one and only one place that people can contact me, and I just ignore Facebook messages, Skype messages, text messages, voicemails, and anything that isn't email. It's amazing.

Doing that should keep your total phone bill down to $20 per month or less. And, with some luck, you might be able to find decent home internet plus tv for under $80, allowing you to be electronified up the yin yang for less than $100 per month.

Another option that might work better for you and your lifestyle, but isn't as cheap, is to just have a phone with a shitload of data on your plan, and use that as a mobile hotspot to do your internet stuff via tablets and laptops and such with at home. The only problem here is that if you stream video it will get outrageously expensive. So, to pull this off and still watch video, you'll have to get DVD's delivered from Netflix just like way back when.

Your phone bill will probably be $200 per month, but I think most people are paying more like $300 per month for phone, internet, and television combined. So still some money saved there. It's perfect for someone who travels a lot, spends little time at home, and doesn't have time nor care for watching much television or online video.

Yet another option is to share internet with one or more of your neighbors. It's ridiculous that everyone has their own internet in an apartment building. It's the epitome of how stupid and inefficient our culture has become. I did live in an apartment once where the neighbors and I shared internet service and it worked out just fine as long as I didn't accidentally hit the wall switch that turned off the internet. When I did the neighbor would come over and be like, "WTF man, I was right in the middle of a movie!"

In fact, *it wasn't until 2013* that I actually, officially paid for my very own internet service (which, again, is a business expense and not a personal one), although I did have an air card from Verizon for a couple years that I could use via a cell signal for about $60 a month with limited data (I wouldn't recommend it).

I don't really care how you trim things up, but there is money to be saved on this stuff, and any true frugal warrior would refuse to perpetually get overcharged for it.

Your Deadly Move: Cut back somewhere in this trinity of electronics bills, and do so with great vengeance against the companies that rip us off on this shit.

TRAVEL

M y two travel tips are incredibly simple, and they are some of the most cost-effective ways at exposing those crouching costs and jabbing them square in the nads.

Even before I started earning a decent online income at age 30 or so, I travelled around six months per year. People referred to me as a "trust-funder," because, as I'm all too happy to tell anyone who will listen, people (other than me) are fucking morons. You don't have to be rich to travel six months per year. You just have to be a heartless frugal warrior.

The other six months of the year I spent working, and when I worked I didn't exactly get paid a ton. I typically made around $14 per hour either working in a restaurant kitchen or as a Wilderness Ranger for the U.S. Forest Service. It was enough to save up $1,000 per month, then I'd go travel for $1,000 per month until I ran out and needed a refill. Rinse and repeat. No trust fund necessary.

How did I do it? Easy. When I travelled outside of the U.S. I went to really cheap countries where I could live like a king for $25 per day or less. And when I travelled inside the U.S. I camped and backpacked (trekking as it's called outside of the U.S.). Also, and this is key, I never kept a place while I was gone. So I didn't have any housing-related bills.

This was also back in the 2000s when I didn't own a computer or a cell phone, had zero debt, and owned the most economical car ever made (a used Geo Metro that I bought outright). I also had a girlfriend that I travelled with on most of those adventures, and she had some money saved up, too. That allowed us to split the cost of things like hotel rooms abroad, which, in the places we visited (Guatemala, Honduras, Mexico, Nepal, Thailand, Vietnam, Cambodia, Laos), averaged $10 per night at most.

The trick, when traveling outside of the country, is to simply go to cheap places (which aren't shitty, they are quite interesting and beautiful and have some of the most attractive, happy, friendly people and best food on the planet for a dollar a plate) and to stay long enough to offset the cost of getting there.

Take Nepal for example. It can cost a ton to get there. Up to $2,000 for a round-trip ticket. But the thing is, Nepal is one of the cheapest countries on earth. The average citizen only makes about one U.S. Dollar per day. Meals are less than $1, hotels are less than $10 and sometimes way cheaper, transportation is very cheap, and you can even go trekking out onto one of several trekking routes for weeks at a time for next to nothing.

You can easily travel for $500 per month or less in Nepal, and that's doing fun stuff, seeing the sites, and eating great food until you're stuffed silly.

Guatemala was one of my favorite frugal warrior hubs as well. The thing to do in Guatemala is to go to Spanish School. They are all over the country—in cities, by the beach, in the mountains—wherever you want to learn. The country is beautiful as well. It looks very much like Hawaii there, with lush vegetation, huge volcanoes, ocean on both sides, rich culture, and ancient ruins.

When I visited, you could get a place to stay, 3 meals a day prepared for you (with amazing displays of unbelievable tropical fruits and other goodies), and 20 hours of one-on-one Spanish instruction alongside one of the world's most beautiful lakes (Lago de Atitlan) for $99 a week.

$99 a fucking week!

It's probably a little more now, but not much. Insane value. And actually getting your own instructor that you spend time with, learning the language, commingling with lots of world travelers all there to do the same thing—it's a vacation with a richness that tops any trip anywhere, and it's cheap beyond belief.

Of course, if you have to travel for several months for these foreign trips to become economical, it means you need the vocational freedom to be able to do that kind of thing. That's why I got into internet business in the first place. I talk about making $100 per day online as a benchmark to feel comfortable "quitting your job" in my QuitN6 course (at www.QuitN6.com), but in reality, if you are desperate to escape the rat race and start living it up like I just described, you can travel the world for $500 per month easily. Being able to live the "digital nomad" type of lifestyle is much more within your reach than you realize. So fucking do something about it!

Now, when it comes to traveling domestically, I can only speak about the U.S. The U.S. has got to be the most amazing country on earth for camping and backpacking. There are several dozen lifetimes worth of trails and wild places with open camping, and there are literally over 100 million acres of public land where you can camp in a tent or RV absolutely free. In just about any National Forest or parcel of land administered by the Bureau of Land Management (BLM), you can open camp for free unless otherwise posted (and it's usually only otherwise posted in the most popular, busy areas, which aren't as fun to spend time at anyway).

Sure, there are stay limits usually of a couple weeks, but it's not enforced very well AT ALL, the punishments aren't severe, and you can drive 100 miles and the public land officials there have never seen you before. You can start all over again.

And then there's backpacking, where you leave your vehicle, pack up everything you need to survive on your back, and go on multi-day hiking adventures in the most pristine places in the world. This is my favorite thing to do. It's some hard fucking work, and it takes a while to develop the skills and hardness required to make the discomforts unnoticeable, but it's well worth the initiation process. There's nothing quite like it.

While it may sound like kind of a hobo's existence, I can't say enough about how magically beautiful and serene life is in unspoiled, natural areas, of which there are an endless abundance in the Western United States and Alaska alone—as well as the amazing Western half of Canada in between them.

And it costs next to nothing. With a wise vehicle purchase, all you HAVE to pay for is car insurance, gas, food, and a little gear to get you set up to have fun out there. Some communication is probably good (cell phone), and nearly everyone (except me) has health insurance. But other than that, you should be good to travel around some of the most gorgeous places on earth for under $1,000 per month.

I spend my days hiking, fishing, tooling around on my inflatable raft in pristine lakes and streams, writing in my journal, reading, cooking, and eating (today I made the most amazing pan-fried focaccia bread with curried potatoes and red beans, damn). And my "work" consists of a daily email check-in when I wake up via satellite hotspot, and writing these here books on my lil' Macbook Air. I don't know if you noticed, but yes I have fun writing!

The only thing I'm missing out here is Mrs. Flogging and her 11-year old offspring. We started this 6+ month excursion together, but she had some serious knee problems and had to fly back to Florida where surgery is covered by her insurance. A bummer indeed. I miss you darling. Go easy on the martinis!

You can live whatever life you want, but I'm clearly a zealot about mine. I would have never known how much I love it if I hadn't done it, so I encourage everyone to work hard to get their lives as free as they need to be in order to give this a try.

Writing this chapter seemed like it took me five minutes. It flew by because the traveling and adventuring I've done, all of which have been made possible by either frugality or an online income or a combination of the two, have been by far the most memorable and exciting experiences of my life.

Even though I know that all this was made possible by my own mindset, determination, and very purposeful decisions to set my life up this way, I still feel beyond blessed to have achieved it. I feel a burning passion, mixed with a little guilt (the 16 free flights I get per year because my dad is a retired airline pilot definitely adds to this!), that drives me to help others do the same.

And that's why I wrote this book. That's why I write books period. I hope something you get from me gives you that spark to make your life congruent with how you'd like it to be.

Your Deadly Move: Stop traveling to places with expensive hotels and eating out at expensive restaurants. You can do that shit at home! Have a real adventure in wild places, or travel somewhere that you can live like royalty for $25 a day—and stay a while.

Housing

Well the secret to cheap housing is easy. Don't have any! I do hope to have a piece of property with a cabin on it in the mountains someday in the not-too-distant future. Between now and then I'll probably be a full on homeless vagabond. Truth be told, I currently sleep in a cargo trailer that I spent about $500 renovating into a camper of sorts, which I lovingly call "The Tramper." Fitting for a tramp like me.

As far as remote cabins are concerned, it's still absurdly cheap in the Rocky Mountain region of the U.S. to buy a small parcel of land and build a cabin—or even buy one prebuilt, buy a yurt, and so on. Once again, a small internet-based income of $1,000 per month would be plenty to survive in a cozy cabin in an area that takes your breath away every time you look out the window. I know that type of living isn't for everyone, but it should be tempting to any true frugal warrior. $15,000 is about all you need in a place like Westcliffe, CO, to get a few acres and a prebuilt cabin. That's some cheap living right there, with some rich views and a short drive to the Sangre de Cristo mountain range—one of the state's most stunning. Just sayin'.

Housing is usually the biggest expense people have in their lifetimes, although, per our prior discussions, real estate is a much better place to have your money than in cash.

I've only owned a home once, and I was a co-owner. The place was purchased for $335,000, I hired contractors to turn the unfinished basement into a sweet bedroom and bathroom for about $20,000—adding 700 livable square feet to the place—and then sold it in under two years from the date it was purchased for $474,000. I split the proceeds with the co-owner who didn't live there (I did), and, all told, I basically ended up living in a nice place for two years and it didn't cost me a dime. I might have even gotten paid a little to live there.

My experience has been that renting = losing money and buying = making money. However, I'm a little spoiled as I sold the place in late summer of 2007 at the absolute peak of the real estate bubble. Coincidence? C'mon now. This is Buck Flogging we're talking about here. I got mad timing baby. It's no accident I bought silver in December of 2008 either. Check those charts to see a master at work!

So, what's the big crouching cost of housing that you didn't know about until Uncle Buck hit you upside the head with it? Well, nothing you haven't already gotten in this book already.

As you know, taking your savings and moving it from cash into real estate is a hidden savings, not a crouching cost, and you can do 80%+ of it with the bank's money. If the value goes up, you win! If the value goes down, you lose a little, but the bank is the one that really has to bite the big one.

Interest rates on home loans are absurdly cheap right now, and they will likely remain that way until inflation goes out of control. Well, technically, inflation, or an increase in the money supply, has already gotten out of control. It just takes a while for the prices of things to reflect that. But it's coming, and I think, all things considered, it looks like a pretty good time to buy a home or some property or both if you've got enough money free to make a down payment on something.

I'd do it myself, but I use my extra money to build businesses (well, websites at least), not homes. It's more fun and the upside is much higher. Plus, I'm too nomadic to buy a home unless it's truly some Jeremiah Johnson shit. Renting has worked for me just fine for a long time, not because renting is a good deal (it isn't, at all), but because renting enables me to quickly move out and travel for many months without any home payments or bills. And that's a mentally-freeing thing I've been willing to overspend a little for over the years.

Although I must say, rents in the area in Florida where I've been living over the last five years have soared in comparison to home prices. It's becoming quite a bit cheaper to buy than rent. Plus, considering that I live in a vacation destination, and with the growing popularity and convenience of sites like vrbo.com and airbnb.com for renting your home while you're away on extended trips, owning a home in my area has become a really attractive prospect—even for a hopeless wanderer like myself. So we shall see. I may become a hardcore home ownership enthusiast a year from now.

While we're on the topic of housing, we should definitely discuss off-grid living, living in areas where there is no cell service (yes, these places still exist, lots of them), and other things that can drop the typical cost of living that you might see in urban areas by 90%. That is, if you pay $500,000 for a 500-square foot apartment in some downtown area, you can probably get something that size for no more than $50,000 in someplace so remote that it's off the grid or out of cell range.

Quite simply, there are pockets where the value you get for your money is insanely better than the norm.

Consider the most expensive place to own a home (that I know of): Aspen, Colorado. The median home price is right around $4 million. You might think they are all huge mansions, but you'd be wrong. Just a small house is $4 million. The big mansions are like $10-100 million. No joke. It's absolutely batshit crazy.

Yet, in the town of Marble, Colorado, a place where I can walk to from Aspen in a day (albeit a VERY long day), you can get the same house, with even better scenery and killer trails right out your door, for $300,000-400,000. Why? Because the town of Marble has dirt roads, no cell service, no grocery store or gas station, no ski areas, and only one restaurant (which is only open four months a year).

Sounds pretty primitive I know (or, if you're like me, it sounds way fucking better than Aspen), but it's amazing there. The town is ten miles from places John Denver sang songs about. Remember the Wilderness

Family, who left New York to live life out in the wild? Filmed, on location, only ten miles from this town. That's just one example, and Marble is still pretty expensive just because of its proximity to Aspen.

There are other towns all over the country that aren't in close proximity to where people like Cher and Don Johnson and Jack Nicholson and Keven Costner have houses. And those places are even cheaper. The reason everyone doesn't live there is because there aren't any good-paying jobs, but we've entered a new era in human civilization where we can work remotely via computer. You better get on it if you expect to earn your frugal black belt!

Lastly, don't rule out the possibility of living outside of the U.S. or whatever expensive-ass country you live in now. Just like with traveling to these places, you can actually live there—at least for most of the year—and live like a celebrity for pennies on the dollar.

I've streamed a few episodes of that Foreign House Hunters show and holy shit do I get a frugal stiffy when they get someone looking at super cheap places that aren't in Europe or North America. I remember in one episode a whole family snagged this huge house on a gorgeous mountainside in Bhutan for like $30 a month!

Seriously though. Get a little location-independent income going and take a hard look at real estate in places like Argentina, Panama, Nicaragua, Thailand, Dominica, and beyond. I hope to hear some fantastic tales of exotic adventures and relocations!

Your Deadly Move: Kick the "Urbs" and Suburbs in the groin, and retreat to a small Buddhist village in the Himalayas where you can meditate about how much money you aren't spending each month on housing.

School

School is much like debt. It can be used to build a great financial future at a relatively low cost, or it can be a complete waste of money that drains the life out of your financial fitness for decades if you don't use the education you paid for to earn more money.

Sadly, most go to college because everyone says you should go to college, they wrack up debt, and then graduate without much more valuable knowledge and experience than than they had when they walked in on the first day.

Put another way, college is a massive, massive expenditure, and it's one that isn't taken very seriously—and it should be taken VERY seriously.

If, at age 18, you went to your parents and said you were thinking about buying a $100,000 car, they would tell you that you were being completely irresponsible with your money right? But they have no problem with you sinking $100,000 into a college education, even if you have no idea what profession you want to apply your degree to going into it.

There's another problem with college, and that is that a college education is very easy to come by. Hundreds of millions of people have college educations, and those educations are fairly common and generic. What I'm saying is that going through the same curriculum as several million others does not give you specialized, valuable skills, information, and expertise. And those valuable skills, information, and expertise is where real value—in the job market and as an entrepreneur—can be found.

If you can't learn this really rare, specialized stuff in college, then where can you get it? You get it by doing your own specialized, specific research, getting job experience from the best at what it is you intend to do (even as a volunteer if you have to), talk to the true experts in the field (they aren't college professors that's for damn sure), and otherwise immerse yourself into something.

Take my experience in the culinary industry as an example...

I grew up with my mom making absolutely everything for me. She was one of those cut-off-the-crust type moms for sure. And when I lived in a house without parents for the first time at age 19, I was totally fucking helpless. I couldn't cook anything, I didn't know how to do my own laundry. Just nothing. Helpless.

But being so helpless gave me this overwhelming urge to become self-sufficient. Cooking soon became my primary hobby.

It was really exhilarating. I couldn't believe how easy it was! I would call up my mom asking her how she made her vegetable soup. I would go get the ingredients, make the shit, and it would taste almost exactly like mom's vegetable soup. Conquering one dish after another gave me tremendous confidence, and every dish I mastered made me curious about how to make two others. I was totally hooked.

So the following year, when I took a year off from money-wasting college and had to get a job, I couldn't help but want to work at a restaurant. I saw a classified ad in the newspaper (for you younger people, a "newspaper" as we called it, was this big awkward mass of low-quality pieces of paper the size of a fucking shower curtain that got ink all over you as you flipped through the pages trying to figure out where the fuck the sports section was) for a line cook at a restaurant I had eaten at as a kid called "Krabloonik."

Krabloonik had some seriously schwanky, high-end, complicated food. The restaurant specialized in serving wild game, with a typical entree in the $50+ range (this was 1998, so more like the equivalent of a $100 entree now). I had no experience. I was obviously way under-qualified for the job, but when I want something I can't help but go after it relentlessly (probably the single greatest key to any and all successes I've had in life).

The chef loved my enthusiasm and excitement for learning, as well as my overwhelmingly abundant and undeniably sincere adoration for the restaurant itself. I had eaten there once as a 4th-grader with my parents and recalled the caribou I was served with food critic-esque vividness.

While he admitted I was certainly not ready to be a line cook, he did hire me right there on the spot (I always got hired on the spot when I applied for jobs... the secret was that the job I was applying for was always the ONLY job on earth I wanted, and my burning desire and exuberance was something no chef could turn away—even if there were no job openings). My role? I was to be "salad bitch." I could hardly contain my excitement. No really, I was totally psyched.

And so, there I went—straight to the very highest echelons of fine-dining. No culinary degree required.

While I was a mere salad bitch, it was only a matter of weeks before the line cook they hired mysteriously disappeared. They were in a bind and had no one to fill that spot. Against their better judgment, they brought me over to the line. They called me "Forcemeat," and were incredibly patient with my preposterously newb-ass questions.

Long story short, I got the ultimate crash course in cooking, and it quickly propelled me through the culinary industry by the seat of my pants. I worked in some of the best restaurants in the U.S., and every chef I worked for was better than EVERY schmuck teaching at any culinary school I promise you that.

Plus, the names of the restaurants I worked at meant far more to my employers than whether or not I attended culinary school. Culinary school meant that I had a basic familiarity with cooking in a restaurant. Actually working at a really good one meant I knew my shit, and could handle the chaos as well.

The one thing that really proved to me that this approach was a vastly superior way to develop valuable skills, knowledge, and expertise was that before I had been cooking even for a full year I was ranked higher and paid more than the culinary grads I had as co-workers, and I even had to train graduates from top culinary schools. And none of them were anywhere near as good as I was. At least not fresh out of school. They were a bunch of fucking stooges.

I again pursued self-study when I launched a career in health and nutrition. I studied my ass off independently for seven years, and as a result, the breadth and depth of my knowledge of the subject matter far exceeds that of 90% of the world's professors, and 99.9% of the students. College students have to write dinky little term papers and a senior thesis. I wrote *over 1 million words* on the subject during my independent studies!

The point here is that, in some (but certainly not all) cases, you are choosing between paying a ton of money for a generic education or getting paid to get a very specific, in-depth, and valuable one.

Really think about whether or not you need to pay for education, or to send your kids to college. Unless they want to be heart surgeons or something else where a college education is mandatory for entering the field, you should encourage them to go straight to the best source and learn directly from pioneers in their area of interest instead.

Never before in human history can we learn so much on our own, all at the click of a button. Professor

Google is far more knowledgeable than most college professors, and his education is always up-to-date.

Nor have there ever been so many amazing opportunities to go and learn, hands on, from the best—or at least communicate with them directly via the internet, watch their YouTube videos, and so forth.

Please think carefully about whether or not you or your kids should be going to college. The feeling like you or your kids must go is probably herd-like mentality creeping in and corralling you into doing something that doesn't make very good sense. Like getting a flu vaccine or a lower back tattoo.

I know it's weird to be the intelligent one, but it's entirely okay to make the smarter choice and have everyone think there is something wrong with you. I've been putting up with it for 20 years, and it's no big deal. I just live in a cargo trailer out in the wild where I hike around in remote areas and don't have to risk seeing any other human beings at all. I'm completely socially normal!

In conclusion, fuck college. Of all the topics in this book, I think nothing rivals college education in terms of costing so much and yielding so little in return—unless you go to Alabama and get student tickets to the football games. That's a different story.

Your Deadly Move: Stop paying so much to learn! Read a couple hundred books, Google your ass off, watch hundreds of hours of YouTube videos, intern or work with the best, practice a shitload in your spare time, and become a knowledgeable expert in your field for pennies compared to college, which doesn't make you an expert in anything other than drunken vomit.

INSURANCE

"*I'm a gamblin' man.*"
I say this every time someone asks me if I want to insure something. I've even trained Mrs. Flogging to say "He's a gamblin' man" as well.

I get protection on absolutely NOTHING. As long as my luck is average, I'll come out on top. After all, the whole game of insurance of any kind is to get everyone to collectively pay more than the major losses of a few.

And, there's the neat kind of insurance that comes free for everyone called Bankruptcy Law. If you do happen to be unlucky and lose all your money due to some health catastrophe or the like, they won't hang you by your thumbs and beat you. At least not in the U.S. Everyone gets a second chance. And sadly, the leading cause of bankruptcy are medical bills by people that HAVE health insurance! So no thanks on the health insurance you buncha fraudsters.

Yes, I don't even have health insurance, and, except for a few months where I felt compelled to "do the right thing" more than a decade ago, I never have. It's even a law in the United States that you have to have health insurance, but even I found a way to give Obama a firm fist between the cheeks.

You see, you have to have health insurance. If you don't, you get fined. But the only way to fine you is to take money out of your annual tax refund. But if you don't get a tax refund (I don't, as I'm self-employed), then you are basically untouchable. I, of course, in my M.C. Hammer-inspired baggy gold pants, am untouchable.

I figure I've saved a couple hundred bucks a month for the last 240 months. Them is sum savins' right there!

And my out-of-pocket healthcare costs during those 240 months has been under $1,500, and that includes some feeble attempts to improve my asthma and lower back pain by seeing an Acupuncturist, a doctor, a Chiropractor, and a handful of other quacks. Of course, none of it did me much good. I just had to learn over time what made my problems better and worse and stop doing the shit that made it worse!

Of course, someday, if I go on to become a sick old fart, I will certainly go get me some health insurance. I do feel, in the back of my mind, that universal healthcare isn't too far away in the United States, so the day I'm so ill that I'm moved to buy health insurance will likely never come, and I will have just saved $50,000 or so by not having health insurance.

What about car insurance? Well, that's a pretty major law in the U.S. You gotta have at least liability coverage or you'll get in big trouble. Full coverage isn't much more expensive, so I do have car insurance. But that's it.

No coverage on my electronic devices, I don't insure the packages I send via the post office, and I don't even have a protective case or a screen cover on my phone. Nothing. I'd rather have a fighting chance to spend $0 extra than pay money to save a little on the off chance things don't go my way.

Occasionally it does indeed bite me in the ass. I bought a $762 plane ticket for someone recently without getting trip protection. Th person couldn't make it, and I was powerless to get a refund or transfer the ticket to someone or anything. The fucking little bastards.

But in the grand scheme of things I save tens of thousands for every time my ass gets bitten with a $762 owie like that.

If you're cool with betting a little money in Vegas, where the odds are stacked against you, then you should definitely be cool with betting money that things in your life won't go catastrophically sour. The odds are stacked very much in your favor.

This is really your decision to make though. If you have toddlers and have had six phones dropped in the toilet in the last four days, then by all means, get full protection on that new phone.

If you suspect you have some major illness that is bound to lead to expensive surgery and treatments, by all means, go get your ass the best health insurance money can buy.

But if you're just a regular person like myself, hey, why not roll the dice and save some money? That's my thinking. You do whatever you're comfortable with, but know that your fear and conservatism is probably going to cost you more than taking a risk and figuratively freeballing your way through life.

Your Deadly Move: Whenever someone asks you if you want to insure something, roundhouse their ass.

Marriage

I admit it. When I saw *The Princess Bride*, I wanted to marry that gorgeous vixen. I felt the same way when I watched *Forrest Gump*. I mean, that Jenny was something else. You can imagine how I felt when I later learned that Jenny and Princess Buttercup were the same person! For like 15 years I had no idea.

More shocking however is that Uncle Rico, Lazlo Hollyfeld, and the Wolfman in Monster Squad (you know, the one that gets kicked in the "nards") are all the same dude! Talk about lifetime achievement award! I hope Jon Gries is in a big old mansion somewheres, in a hot tub, soaking it up with his soul mate. I really do.

And most shocking of all is that when my sister got married (the first time), my dad dropped roughly $40,000 on the wedding. And he didn't even get Franc and his assistant Howard Weinstein to help plan the thing!

Sorry, I'm going overboard with the '80s movie references. It isn't the first time and it won't be the last.

Damn, that just reminds me of how classic the movie *Overboard* is, which, coincidentally, is about a woman who is much happier poor than rich. "Arturo! Catarina!"

Seriously, weddings are super expensive. And as much as I'd like to make this chapter about saving money on the cake and picking the right spot for a groovy yet affordable reception, I really can't just bite my tongue on this one...

Don't fucking get married! Seriously, it's not the fucking 1800's anymore you fucking imbecile!

Sure, I got wrapped up in the whole romance of marriage back when I was a teenager and hadn't yet located the critical thinking region of my brain. I was operating on autopilot back then, a pure product of my social programming—most of it delivered through '80s films and music videos.

And I love '80s films and music videos, don't get me wrong. But that cheesy happily-ever-after marriage bullshit is for amusement. It's not real. You don't have to get married just like I don't have to go to Japan and fight to the death like Daniel LaRusso to bang cute Asian girls.

It's hard to admit, but I actually proposed to my high school girlfriend and gave her a "promise ring" before I went off to college. So ridiculous. We had nothing in common, and I don't even think we were that attracted to each other. We were more just living out childhood fantasies that we gathered from movies (me) and books (her). She was so obsessed with the marriage idea she didn't even want to have sex before getting married! Fortunately I was persuasive enough to convince her that as long as I didn't ejaculate inside her, that it didn't count as sex, and I got to blow at least a few loads on her stomach—but not the few PER

DAY that my body strongly tried to convince me to do at that age (fortunately, now that I'm 38, my sex drive has cooled off to a mere twice per day...ladies).

Never again.

Marriage is a dumb, unrealistic, antiquated, hoaky religious practice that has no place in the 21st century, and if you are thinking about getting married, then I suggest you turn your comatose brain on before it's too late. Shit, I think I was the only person adamantly protesting gay marriage that actually liked gay people and wanted to do them a favor!

If you're already married, well, make the best of it you can I guess. We all make mistakes, it's how we deal with them that separates the winners from the losers in life.

If you don't think marriage is ridiculous, and that people who believe in it strongly aren't mental cripples, then take this recent real-life example:

My girlfriend (who I call Mrs. Flogging, because I can), and I recently had to spend some time apart. I really wanted to be out in the West hiking, and she did too, but her knee is all fucked up. So she went back to Florida to get work done on it while I stayed.

A family member of hers said the following, because she thought we like broke up or something,

"Well if he really loved her he would have married her by now."

To prove my point, this was said by someone who got knocked up at 15 by her first boyfriend, got married shortly thereafter, and now has six fucking kids. I can almost hear the banjo music playing in the background.

Needless to say, she's also the type that jolts up from the table at Thanksgiving and cleans the dishes like she's on speed so that she can be the first in line at Target on Black Friday.

Buck don't Black Friday, okay people.

But I assure you I do really love my girlfriend (and have really loved all my girlfriends) even though we're not married and even though I refuse to breed with her (she's not into breeding or marriage either). In fact, until we had to painfully part ways just a while ago, the longest we've been apart in the last four years is three hours. Some say we're crazy. What do they know? Put your arms around me baby, don't ever let go.

My huge marriage tangent aside, I encourage everyone reading this to strongly consider an unwed life. I know there are tax benefits to being married, but they aren't that significant in most scenarios. I claim Head of Household and do just as well.

Savings on the cost of actually getting married (which most are doing once every decade or two these days) outweigh a lot of tax savings, and cost of divorce, the most likely outcome of marriage, can be unfathomably brutal.

So just don't. You'll save a ton of money.

Back to the movie *Overboard*, you know the main characters, Kurt Russell and Goldie Hawn, never got married right? Goldie was interviewed about why she never wanted to get married, and Norm McDonald reported about it on Saturday Night Live's news segment, saying that he was planning on discussing more details about Goldie in the book he was working on, called "The Greatest Woman Who Ever Lived." Haha.

Oh, and if you don't get married, odds are you'll be less likely to breed as well. The sophistication of a society is very well-reflected in the birth rate. The lower a nation's birth rate, the smarter, more conscious, more empowered, and more wealthy are its citizens. Typically. And there are no greater savings to be had than not having kids, or at least having only one or two like smart couples typically do.

Your Deadly Move: Don't do the deed and don't breed!

Bonus Move

Lastly, let me also throw out the suggestion to kick all of your vices. Vices are expensive, stealthfully adding up to thousands, tens of thousands, and even hundreds of thousands of dollars over decades.

Your first reaction may be to whine and moan at me or even call me a prude. Fuck you. Your banter with the Starbucks cashier about how every clumsy mistake you make is because of a caffeine deficiency isn't funny. It's woefully unoriginal. You're a weak, little bitch.

Nah, you're not weak for having vices, just stupid.

The thing about addictive substances and activities is that they literally create the symptom that they provide relief from. As you become more and more addicted, it becomes increasingly pronounced. You won't be able to produce energy without caffeine. You won't be able to feel joy without alcohol. You'll start stressing out about something without nicotine. You won't be able to be aroused sexually without watching a half dozen lesbians taking turns fucking a mule. And so on.

To once again reference and '80s movie, the only way to win the game is not to play.

You don't have to live in a commune or wear magical underwear to live free of vices. I don't wear any underwear at all. And you don't have to be particularly strong or have superhuman willpower either. The desire for a "fix" of some kind disappears pretty quickly if you eat well (as in consistently eat enough, without weird food restrictions), sleep well, and live well.

Just had to throw that out there. I've saved ungodly amounts of money by avoiding costly vices throughout the course of my life. I didn't do it to save money, I've just always had an extreme aversion to mind-altering substances—almost a phobia in fact. That phobia has benefited me tremendously in the wallet area, and I'd love to see you enjoy similar savings, as well as the smugness that comes without having any vices.

CONCLUSION

While many of you will write much of what's in this book off as impractical and extreme, I challenge you not to. Really think about just how much your social and cultural programming has shaped your life. Is that really what you want to be making the big decisions on how you exist in this world? Or is there something more spirited, adventurous, creative, and daring than that inside you? Do you have those yearnings to do something wild and crazy just for the sake of adding contrast to a life where one day blends in with the next as years pass by undetected? I hope so.

To be honest, I don't care all that much about what you do with your money. Yes, I want you to spend your money responsibly and ethically. I don't want you abusing power and resources like so many do just because they can. In that sense, I hope you aren't wasteful.

What I really want, and I'm sure you've picked up on this by now, is for you to live a rich and fulfilling life with a variety of interesting and enlivening experiences. I want you to break free from the life template that we've been handed since birth and create your own life, completely from scratch, with your own unclouded vision of what you'd like it to be.

We live in a time of many great paradoxes. We are more connected than we've ever been as a species, yet never before have we been so disconnected from many of the most basic human experiences. We live in a time where there is an absolutely never-ending stream of stimulation, yet never before have so many lived dull, empty lives. We live in a time where we've never been busier, yet so many of us feel completely and utterly restless and bored.

Break free! If it's the quest for frugality that is your portal into a more unique and meaningful life, great. If not, find something else to be that catalyst.

I'm here to help you with the tools, knowledge, and experience I've amassed. Let me know what I can do.

Your partner in progress,

The Flogfather

Your Deadly Move: Change at least one thing about your life that you aren't happy with immediately. Oh, and write a review for this fucking book saying how awesome it was.

Publish Yourself

Want to have fun writing and publishing your own work, but you're not sure where to start? Visit Archangel Ink and sign up for my partner Rob Archangel's FREE self-publishing report to find out what you need to do to launch your writing career.

Go to www.archangelink.com/report to find out more.

About Buck

Buck Flogging is an author and creator of more than a half dozen successful websites since 2014, including BuckBooks.net, Goodriter.com, DigitalFreedom.Academy, QuitN6.com, and several others--each launched to instant success (from $2,000-60,000 in their first month).

Success didn't always come easily for Buck though, as it took him a long and painful five years of working up to 100 hours per week online just to achieve a full-time living.

Buck understands both the intensity of the desire we all share to increase our personal freedom through internet-based income, as well as how daunting it can be to reach success when starting at ground zero. That's why he created a unique and simplified approach to quick internet success with his Quit Your Job in 6 Months Internet Business Course (QuitN6 for short).

Whether you aspire to sell physical or digital products, be an author, freelancer, blogger, podcaster, instructor, coach, or consultant online, the QuitN6 course can help you avoid major rookie mistakes that can delay or even destroy your chances of achieving success.

Learn more at www.QuitN6.com

www.ingramcontent.com/pod-product-compliance
Lightning Source LLC
Chambersburg PA
CBHW020601030426
42337CB00013B/1161